THE QUEST
A Guide to the Job Interview

By the Faculty in Effective Speaking
Cazenovia College

Kathryn Barbour, Ph.D.
Fredric Berg, Ph.D.
Maryrose Eannace
John Robert Greene, Ph.D.
Mary Jean Hessig
Margot Papworth
Carol Radin
Edward Rezny
John Suarez

KENDALL/HUNT PUBLISHING COMPANY
2460 Kerper Boulevard P.O. Box 539 Dubuque, Iowa 52004-0539

Dedicated to our Students.

Cover photographs by Gene Gissin Photography, Cazenovia, New York.

Copyright ©1991 by Kendall/Hunt Publishing Company

ISBN 0-8403-6984-0

All rights reserved. No part of this publication may be reproduced, stored in a retrieval system, or transmitted, in any form or by any means, electronic, mechanical, photocopying, recording, or otherwise, without the prior written permission of the copyright owner.

Printed in the United States of America
10 9 8 7 6 5 4 3 2 1

CONTENTS

Acknowledgements .... *vii*

PART ONE: **How to Get an Interview**

CHAPTER 1 — Anyone Can Get a Job if a Job is All You Want: GETTING STARTED 3

CHAPTER 2 — I Found My Job Through My Uncle's Girlfriend's Brother's Butcher's Daughter WHERE TO LOOK FOR A JOB 7

CHAPTER 3 — K.I.S.S. (Keep It Simple, Students) WRITING YOUR RESUME 11

CHAPTER 4 — Close Encounters of the First Kind THE COVER LETTER 21

CHAPTER 5 — Street Maps and Mind Maps Sold Here PRE-INTERVIEW PREPARATION 27

PART TWO: **The Type of Person Who Gets the Job: The Empowered Interviewee**

CHAPTER 6 — A Little Bit of an 'Edge' NERVES 33

CHAPTER 7 — You Are What You Wear WHAT TO WEAR 37

CHAPTER 8 — How You Say "I Want The Job" EMPOWERMENT 41

CHAPTER 9 — TELLING THE TRUTH 43

PART THREE: The Heart of the Matter: The Questions and How You Answer Them

CHAPTER 10	You Never Get a Second Chance to Make That First Impression THAT FIRST ONE MINUTE	47
CHAPTER 11	Turnabout, Fair Play WHAT THE INTERVIEWER IS THINKING	51
CHAPTER 12	This is *Not* A Multiple Choice Exam HOW TO RESPOND TO *ANY* QUESTION	55
CAHPTER 13	Now, Tell Me About Yourself STRATEGIES FOR OFTEN ASKED QUESTIONS	57
CHAPTER 14	Know Before You Go! CONTROLLING ILLEGAL QUESTIONS	61
CHAPTER 15	"Uh, Excuse Me . . . But About the Money?" THE QUESTION OF SALARY	63
CHAPTER 16	Body Talk Speaks Louder Than Words NON VERBAL COMMUNICATION	67
CHAPTER 17	I'm Deciding on *You*, Too! "NOW, DO *YOU* HAVE ANY QUESTIONS?"	69
CHAPTER 18	Applying the Brakes HOW TO SAVE IT WHEN IT'S GOING DOWNHILL	71

PART FOUR: After the Interview

CHAPTER 19	Prompt and Circumstance STEPS TO BE TAKEN IMMEDIATELY	75
CHAPTER 20	Congratulations . . . But Hold the Phone! WHAT IF YOU'RE OFFERED THE JOB?	77
CHAPTER 21	You *Can* Win for Losin'! WHAT IF YOU'RE *NOT* OFFERED THE JOB?	79

PART FIVE:	**Twists, Tricks, and Special Cases**	
CHAPTER 22	S.A.T.'s, or Y.O.U.? THE COLLEGE TRANSFER INTERVIEW	85
CHAPTER 23	Fake? THE 'MOCK,' OR CLASSROOM INTERVIEW	87
CHAPTER 24	Abridged Over Troubled Waters USING AN ART PORTFOLIO	89
CHAPTER 25	A LIST OF OUR MOST VALUABLE HINTS	93
INDEX		95
READER EVALUATION FORM		97

ACKNOWLEDGEMENTS

No book is written in a vacuum. People helped us finish this work, and we would be remiss if we did not thank them.

First we would like to thank each other. This was a collaborative effort, and we spent the better part of a year reading each others work, analyzing it, testing it in our classes, and offering our criticism. We weren't always kind to each other's ideas, but our comments to each other made for a better book. We made a pretty good team.

Our spouses, significant others, children, and other members of our families gave us the time to work, and the distance to work *right*.

The faculty and administration of Cazenovia College supported our efforts at every turn. Let us acknowledge the special contributions to this volume of college President Steven Schneeweiss, Vice President Carolyn B. Ware, Jo Buffalo, Faith Dickenson, and Virginia Solomon. Particular thanks go to Professor Jennifer Ferguson, who read the draft in its entirety, and made helpful comments.

Written for students, and written with the *help of* students. Thanks to Jennifer George, Mary Roach, and Thyda Ros, who formed a seminar for us which offered the student viewpoint on the draft. Also a million thanks to our student typists—Sean Bowen, Christine Caffrey, Heather Clark, Wendy Payano, and Janet Stiles.

Photo Credits are with Gene Gissin Photography, Cazenovia, New York.

Finally, to our students—those whom we have taught, and those who will learn something from this book. It is to you that this book is dedicated, as it should be. We wrote this for you, and few things have given us more pleasure as professors. Find your measure of success, earn it, and we will have succeeded as teachers.

Cazenovia College
Cazenovia, NY

PART ONE

How to Get an Interview

CHAPTER 1

Anyone Can Get a Job if a Job Is All You Want

Getting Started

This is a true story. My wife has a cousin named Larry, who graduated high school in the late 1970's. Although he knew he wanted to go to college, Larry had no particular job path in mind; no idea as to what he wanted to be "when he grew up." But he did have a passion: Larry loved to play golf. Unfortunately, he knew he wasn't good enough to become a top professional golfer and make a living at the sport. Everybody told him, "just get a good job, you can play golf on the weekends," but the idea of being cooped up in an office five days a week and out on the links only two days just didn't cut it with Larry. So, he sat down and started to think his situation through:

> Who plays golf? Golf pros and weekend duffers. I'm not good enough to be a star, club pros don't last forever, and I want more than the weekend. Let's try a different approach. Where do people play golf? On golf courses. Where are these courses? Everywhere. What do you need to have a golf course? Land, a designer, a lawn mower, someone to run the place . . . (picture the little light bulb coming on over his head). How would I get to be one of the people who runs a golf course?

To make a long story short, Larry discovered a college that gives a degree in golf course management (no kidding!), got one, and discovered upon graduation that not only would someone hire him to do what he loves to do (he gets to play golf everyday), but, since there are golf courses everywhere, he also had his choice of where he wanted to live.

The point? *It's easy to get a job, if all you want is a job.* But with a little thought and planning, you can set yourself on the path of finding a job that fulfills you, interests you, challenges you and rewards you financially and personally—in short, a career. Nobody likes looking for a job, but most people go about it in such a way that the job they'll probably land is one they won't want to keep very long, and so they set themselves up to be out looking for a job again before too long. (Or even worse, they set themselves up in a job they're unhappy with and stay there rather than face another job hunt.) So, before we even get into want ads, resumes, and interviews, let's discuss how you know what it is you want in the first place.

Begin by asking yourself a few simple and basic questions. First of all, *what are your career goals?* In the long term, do you have a clearly defined goal towards which you are working? (If you do, you can skip to want ads and resumes, etc.) If not, start to think like Larry: what are your *interests*; what do you like to do; is there any way someone else might pay you to follow these interests? For example, do you love to travel? Would you like to get paid to do so? Have you ever arranged a trip through a travel agent? Did you know that travel agents get to travel free to check out the hotels and restaurants and sights and rate them? Or, do you really love animals, yet do you know that veterinary school is harder to get into than medical school? Have you ever considered how veterinarians keep up to date on food, medicines, procedures, equipment, etc.? Companies hire and train salespeople to visit vets and combine a sales pitch with product education.

Nothing coming to mind? Well, do you have a *lifestyle* you aspire to, and more importantly, how much does it cost? Do you want to live by the ocean; live in the big city; work at your own schedule; work with people with certain interests; not have any worries or responsibilities? What kinds of work could support these ambitions, and which of those kinds of work do you feel you might have an interest in or aptitude for?

If you're still having trouble with long term goals, try thinking in the short term instead. Ask yourself four questions. First, *what do I want to do now*; given your choice, what sounds like the perfect job? This question obviously has two answers—one realistic and one idealized. Looking at both, what are the common elements? What kinds of work might include those elements? For example, if you would ideally like to design clothing, but the only fashion related jobs you know of are as a display designer or as a buyer trainee, you might initially see the display design position as closest to your long range goals. Look at it more closely, though, and you will see that the autonomy, the entrepreneurial business approach, and the freedom to create will be more within your reach from the initially less glamorous buyer's position. Not only will that expose you to the business side of fashion, but it will enable you to make the contacts which could, eventually, lead to Seventh Avenue.

The second question is *what must I earn?* This question also has two answers. The first is based on financial reality: what do you absolutely need to earn in order to live? Remember, this includes necessities (rent, utilities, food, insurance, clothing) and luxuries (entertainment, travel). The second answer is based upon your self-esteem: what value do you put on your sense of self, your education, and your pride? Specifically, what amount would feel satisfying based on what others are earning, what you've done to compete in the market place, and the kind of life you want to live now.

Once the two basic needs of material and spiritual well-being are fulfilled, the third question is *what do you hope to get out of a job?* Among the answers to this include: a sense of competency, a social network, collegiality, enhanced self-esteem, and prestige in the eyes of others. And you must also ask yourself the fourth question, which is really the opposite side of question three: *what type of work will you definitely turn down?*

Okay, you've asked yourself all these questions and you're still not sure. Don't panic; at the age of 19 or 20, very few people are 100% certain of their life goals. But keep this in mind: while it's hard to choose one door out of all those available to you, life involves making choices and accepting the limits of those choices—you can't be everything. *Choose the best fit available now,* and remember that a career change at age thirty, while difficult, is better than a thirty-year career you hate.

Hints to Remember

- It's easier to find something when you know what you're looking for. Make your decisions ahead of time.
- Look for a career opportunity, not just a job.
- Don't quit on yourself. There are many kinds of employment opportunities out there—find a good fit.

CHAPTER 2

I Found My Job Through My Uncle's Girlfriend's Brother's Butcher's Daughter

Where to Look for a Job

Let's start with the obvious places. *Read the want ads* in your local newspaper and/or in the local newspapers of areas you might be interested in relocating to. With practice, you can learn to read want ads for any hidden messages about the job. For example, "fast paced, exciting environment..." can be translated as, "expect to work more than 40 hours a week." "Potential for rapid growth..." should be read as, "We're going to pay you less to start to see if you can make it." You can also learn to separate the actual company ads from the employment agency ads. In most states, agencies have to list themselves as such, but the words "fee paid" or "no fee" are giveaways, and you'll also learn the names of the major agencies in your area by some quick comparison—while it's not likely that a single company would advertise for retail staff, medical assistants, and computer repair technicians, an agency will.

However, don't just read the employment section of the newspaper. *Read the business section as well* and look for companies that are changing or growing (or shrinking, for that matter—companies often look for entry level people to replace more expensive employees or to replace change-resistant employees). It can't hurt to have your resume in before they start advertising.

Use your college placement or recruitment office. Often, employers will bypass the newspapers if they are looking for college graduates, feeling that the best place to find future college grads is in college. Be sure to know when company *recruiters* will be on your campus, and be ready both to ask and answer questions. Another source to check out is your local city or state employment service—after all, you're paying for them—but be aware that these offices tend to offer the sort of job that is so unsatisfactory that it will only be filled by those who must accept it or lose their benefits.

The final obvious source of jobs is a *private employment agency*. Most of these companies are fee paid by the employer. Agency contracts are legally binding, so always ask to see it in writing, and do not ever sign anything you do not understand. When you want to believe that they'll find the perfect job for you, it's easy to go along with their agenda rather than your own. Agencies can be very helpful, but be a smart consumer and be sure you know what you're agreeing to.

However, as good and useful as all these are, one of, if not the best sources of jobs is your own personal network of family, friends and acquaintances. Your cousin Sam may not have a job for you, but if he knows you're looking he can mention it to his friend Kate, who tells her co-worker Bob, who tells his grocer Frank, whose sister Mary owns a company and would be interested in talking to you about a job opening she has. This is called *networking*, and is possibly the most effective way to go about a job search.

There are two other points to mention here, both of which relate to determining whether or not to go after a specific job. First, how can you find out more about a company you're interested in? The easiest way is to let the company tell you about itself—if the business section of your school or city library doesn't have a copy of the company's annual report, you can usually get one just by calling the switchboard and asking to have one sent to you. In addition, there are many directories that contain information on companies, including *The National Directory of Advertisers*, *Standard and Poors*, *The Thomas Register*, and directories published by local or regional Chambers of Commerce. (While there is usually a fee for Chamber of Commerce directories, the others should also be available in the business section of any good library). Finally, do not neglect your network of friends and family in doing your research. Someone you or someone else knows may work for the company you're interested in—ask!

The second point is a major problem for those just starting out in the job market; most jobs need experience, so how can you compete? Well, if the job actually, honestly needs experience, write it off. But, you can put the best face on your lack of experience and try to make it work for you. In exploring a job for which you have some related skills but no direct experience, try emphasizing your willingness to learn, your energy and openness, and your commitment to the company. (The last is important; after all, why should they train you if you're going to take the training and run?) In addition, keep in mind that in a tight job market, an entry level worker costs a lot less than an experienced worker.

Hints to Remember

- Even if you have no experience, your education and willingness to work are assets.
- If it sounds too good to be true, it almost certainly is!
- Do your homework—you only get one chance to make a first impression!

CHAPTER 3

K.I.S.S. (Keep it Simple, Students)

Writing Your Resume

A resume is a marketing document, a planned presentation of your skills and experience, designed to interest the reader and provoke an interview. *A RESUME WILL NOT GET YOU A JOB. It may, however, get you the interview. If you are preparing your first resume, ask yourself the following questions:*

1. What work have I done or what experience do I have that involves work skills?

Have you been a summer camp counselor, peer tutor, clerk, fast food worker, stable hand, Crisis Center volunteer, baby sitter, political campaign worker, college newspaper reporter (or editor, photographer, paste-up person), club president, charity fund raising volunteer, etc.?

2. What does this experience say about me that an employer needs to know?

Does it show me to be reliable, hard-working, organized, responsible, active, literate, serious about my career, able to work under stress, detail-oriented, ambitious, etc.?

3. What skills, experience, or aptitude do I have that is "special?"

Can I use or program a personal computer, speak or read another language/s, perform numerical tasks easily, keep and balance a ledger, draw or perform other graphic arts work, do photography on a better than snapshot level, read and/or draw blueprints, present well in front of a group, etc.?

When you sit down to write your resume, keep in mind that business people are generally conservative, at least in matters pertaining to their business, so choose a standard, conservative presentation: white or off white paper, facts and not opinions, brief and to the point.

Remember that a resume must answer the following questions for the reader:

1. How can they reach you?

Give your name, address and phone number. (If you are still in college, you may want to give both your home and college addresses and phones).

2. What are you looking for?

Formulate a clear, concise and comprehensible objective, including the level of job and the field of interest. Avoid phrases such as "a challenging position" (who doesn't want a challenging job?) and "in a growing (or well-managed, or financially secure) company" (do you expect to see the books before you make a decision; would you turn down a mature, stable business?).

3. What work experience do you have?

List it in a straightforward, reverse-chronological presentation and include any specifics that reflect well on you. (For example, did you receive a promotion; handle money; have responsibility for others; create or improve the methods of operation?) Remember, even something as ordinary as babysitting can appear impressive if you paint it so: did you sit for special children, have additional household responsibilities?

4. What academic training do you have?

Again, in reverse-chronological order, list only the high school you graduated from and every college you have attended, with the degree obtained in each. Include academic honors, but be sure they are honors (i.e.: don't list your grade point average if it's below a 3.0). If you are still in school, specify when you *expect* to graduate and with what degree.

5. What awards and honors have you received, either in school or in your community?

To what organizations do you belong and what titles have you held? With what local or national groups are you affiliated? (Companies like to know that you are a joiner, it shows that you are a "team" player). What specific skills and interests do you have? Give clear, concise statements of fact.

There are also two items that many people put on their resume that *simply do not belong*:

1. Never include references to salary, either what you have made or what you are hoping to make.

You neither want to price yourself out of the market, nor undercut yourself. The time to bring up salary is only after you have been offered the job.[1]

2. You may state that references are available upon request, although this really isn't necessary as all employers assume you have references and will produce them when needed. But you should *never send your references along with a resume*.

By sending them out wholesale, you not only lose control of the courtesy (and necessity) of notifying your references that they will be contacted and by whom, you also violate their privacy. As with salary information, the correct time and place for such a request is after a mutual interest is established, not before. You should have at least three references prepared, which means that you should have asked these people if they are willing to serve as references, you should have reviewed your resume and qualifications with them in person or on the telephone, you should have a typed list of contact information to supply to the interviewer if asked, and you should have called each of these references as soon as you release this list. Also, keep in mind that a reference, properly, is someone who knows you in a capacity to judge your potential as a worker. This might include your most recent ex-boss, an academic advisor, a colleague from a club or organization, a paid staffer at an agency where you have worked as a volunteer, etc. This should not include—unless they fit one of these other categories—your friends, family, pastors, or anyone else whose knowledge of you is not pertinent to you as a worker.

Remember that this is a resume, not the great American novel. Tell the truth, tell it clearly, and remember that you are not expected to have earned the Nobel Peace Prize by the age of twenty. Get lots of feedback on your resume, but realize that everyone has read a different Bible on resume writing. Use your judgement and keep in mind that the resume will be out

---

1. For more hints on handling the question of Salary, see Cahpter 15.

there representing you—not your best friend's father. *Proof it* for typos, grammatical heresies (this is their first impression of you and as such it must be error free) and general readability. Many resumes are useless, save as a sleeping aid. Don't let yours be one of them.

Hints to Remember

- Present the best description of your work history that you can, but always be factual.
- Neatness counts!
- Brevity is best—effective business communications are to the point. It's a good habit—start now!

For Your Consideration:
Three Examples of Resumes

What follows are three examples of resumes. While the names are fictitious, the layouts resemble those which have actually been used by our students as they prepare their resume for their interviews.

Do to these what interviewers do to theirs—*like you were a teacher correcting a paper, use a red pencil to correct these resumes.* Pick out the strengths, weaknesses, and the poor strategies in each.

As you no doubt noticed after reading the previous chapter, *none of these resumes are perfect.* But here's a hint—we believe that the first one is the best (a grade of B+/A-), the second one has problems (a low C-), and the third one is pretty poor (a solid F)!

Resume 1

JANE SMITH

44 Elm Street
Centraltown, NY 11111
(123) 456-7890

Bell Hall #101
Northern State College
Middleville, MN 55555
(098) 765-4321

Objective:
   An entry level position in the field of Child Care

Education:
   1990-Present: Northern State College, Middleville, MN 55555
   AA Degree in Child Services, expected May 1991

   1986-1990: Centraltown High School, Centraltown, NY 11111
   Regents Diploma; Dean's List; 3.8 Average (out of 4.0)

Experience:
   Summers 1989 and 1990: Centraltown Day Care Center
   Worked as a Teacher's Aide-responsible for assisting teacher of 7 preschoolers with day to day activities and special trips. Devised special buddy system for trips.

   1987-1989: Pete's Market, 7 Main Street, Centraltown, NY 11111
   Began as Stock Clerk and Cashier, promoted to Assistant Weekend Manager with responsibility for cash receipts and management of five employees.

   1987-Present: Baby Sitter
   Have sat for numerous children in Centraltown, including a handicapped child and a retarded child.

Honors and Awards:
   New York State Regents Scholarship Winner-1990

Activities:
    Centraltown High School Volleyball team-Voted Most Valuable Player, 1987 and 1988.
    Centraltown High School Drama Club
    Northern State College Peer Tutoring Service

Affiliations:
    Phi Theta Kappa Honor Society, American Church Youth Association

Interests:
    Sports, Travel

Skills:
    Computers-Lotus, Word Perfect 5.0, Multimate

References:
    Available Upon Request.

Resume 2

JOHN ADAM DOE

567 Main Street
Mytown, Arizona 88888
(000) 000-0000

OBJECTIVE

An entry level position in retail or business management.

EDUCATION

5/91 A.S. in Accounting, Local Community College, Mytown, AZ

6/90 High School Diploma, Central High School, Mytown, AZ

EXPERIENCE

6/87-5/91 Summer and After School positions in fast food stores, lawn care, Summer-in-the-Park Activity Programs for Children, and Babysitting.

PERSONAL

Born: 5/8/71 Single Excellent Health Active in Jogging and Swimming

Resume 3

Harvey Hendricks
123 Northeast West Street
Everytown, OH, 33333

OBJECTIVE: A challenging career in my field which will enable me to use my training and expertise and which will properly reimburse me.

EDUCATION:
    3 Years of High School
    2 Years of College - 2.65 Grade Average

EXPERIENCE:
    June 1982-March 1985 -   Pete's Laundry and Conch Fritter Shop—
                                        Salary - $5.75/hour

    March 1985-April 1985 -   Unemployed

    May 1985-September 1989 - General Motors Corporation, Detroit
                                          President and Chief Executive Officer
                                          -Implemented new management policy resulting in increased profits
                                          -Introduced new five wheel car, boosting company's sales 300%
                                          -fired because I told the boss I didn't like his face

    October 1989-Present -   Independent House Painter

REFERENCES:
    Pete, 123 Main Street, Everytown, OH 33333 (098)-765-4321
    Mrs. H. Hendricks (My Mother),123 Northeast West Street, Everytown, OH, 33333

I am not interested in any job that pays less than $500 per week.

CHAPTER 4

Close Encounters of the First Kind

The Cover Letter

You've spent weeks writing, editing, inputting, and printing the perfect resume. When you're finally done, you quickly tack on a cover letter and confidently send them off to your dream company. The firm rejects you immediately. What went wrong? There's a good possibility the firm never even bothered to read your resume; they may have instantly decided that you were not a good candidate merely from reading your hastily prepared cover letter. *Cover letters are usually the first opportunity we have to introduce ourselves to a firm.* Why blow that chance by being careless?

A cover letter is not just a note which tells a firm you've enclosed a resume; it's a critical opportunity to show a firm you're the kind of employee they're looking for. In that regard, many of the rules for cover letters are the same as discussed in the previous chapter on preparing resumes.

Companies want professional employees. You will not appear very professional if your cover letter contains mistakes in spelling, punctuation, or grammar. Be as careful proofreading and editing it as you were when you worked on your resume. Restrict your cover letter to *one page, and type it* on good quality 8 1/2" by 11" paper. If you've printed your resume on colored stock, try to use the same paper for your cover letter. If a print shop prepared your resume, purchase extra copies of that stock to use for your cover letters.

Companies want employees who show initiative. Don't prepare a form letter and send it out to every firm you write to; tailor each cover letter to a specific firm. Don't be satisfied to address the letter, "To Whom It May Concern," because that gives the impression that you weren't concerned. Similarly, don't blindly address the letter, "Dear Sir," because there's a good chance the person you're writing to is a woman.

You should always direct your letter to a particular person at a firm. (The only exception is if the ad doesn't say who the firm is and merely gives a box number to write to.) If you are responding to an ad which tells you to write to the Vice President of Marketing, you can easily find out the name of that person by calling up the firm and asking. Personalizing the letter that way sets you apart from the respondents who simply write "Dear Vice President of Marketing." But be sure to ask how to spell the name properly; you will appear careless if you write to "Jack Anderson" if it's really "Jacques Anderssen."

If you want to write to a firm's Art Director and discover the person's name is Chris Jones, do not assume it is a man and write, "Dear Mr. Jones"; if Chris is a woman, she will not react favorably when she gets your letter. Furthermore, if you learn Chris is a woman, do not write, "Dear Miss Jones" or "Dear Mrs. Jones;" you never want to jump to conclusions. In the business world, "Dear Ms. Jones" is preferred.

Companies want organized employees, so it's important that your cover letter is well organized...

- *Begin with an attention-getting introduction.* In your first paragraph, name the specific position you are applying for and how you learned of the opening. If you saw an ad, state the date and name of the publication (and underline the publication's name). If a friend of yours who works for the firm told you, be sure to mention it immediately (assuming, of course, that your friend is well respected by the person you're writing to). Another way to gain a reader's attention is to include facts that you learned while researching the company.

- *The body of the letter* should show the reader that you have the skills and characteristics the firm wants. Companies are not interested in what they can do for you; they want to know what you can do for them. Do not merely repeat word-for-word what is listed on your resume; tailor your information to the specific job and the specific firm. If the ad says the person must be creative, discuss your innovations. If the person must be able to work in a high-pressured environment, discuss the accomplishments you achieved under heavy deadline pressure. It's important to emphasize your belief that your experience, intelligence or interest can benefit the firm. But don't be arrogant. Instead of saying, "I'm the perfect person for the job," say instead, "My experience editing the college newspaper enabled me to hone my written communication skills."

- *In your closing paragraph*, summarize what you can offer the firm, express your desire to discuss the opening with them further, indicate where and when you can be reached if they have any questions or would like to arrange an interview, and thank them for their cooperation. If you will still be living in your dorm through May 20, and at your home after that date, explain that. Recruiters will try to contact you once or twice, then they will call someone else. *Make sure you're easy to contact* (you could always buy an answering machine). Finally, thank them for their consideration.

Applying these principles will help ensure that your cover letter works for you, not against you. Most importantly, it may help you pass the first close encounter and move on to the next stage of the process—planning for the actual interview.

Hints to Remember

- Always send a cover letter whenever you send a resume.
- Carefully prepare a well-organized, professional cover letter.
- Address the cover letter to the appropriate individual.
- Detail accomplishments that match specific job requirements.
- Make it as easy as possible for the recruiter to contact you.

A Sample Cover Letter

July 12, 1992

                                      758 Positive Place
                                      Cazenovia, NY 13035
                                      (315) 555-1212

Ms. Lorna Fried
General Manager
Gypsy G
1819 Henderson Plaza
Baldwinsville, New York 13027

Dear Ms. Fried:

Please consider this letter and enclosure as my application for the position of Design Assistant, as advertised in the July 12, 1991 edition of the Syracuse *Herald-American*.

Understanding of market niche, attention to detail, and clever use of fabric are three qualities which characterize my approach to fashion design.

An important starting point for me in the design of any article of clothing is a clear understanding of what the intended consumer wants. Not only does this increase the chances of developing a successful product from a sales perspective, but it also adds the creative challenge in the design process.

Fabric choices are increasing during this era of expanding technology. Choosing and using new—as well as traditional—fabrics to cut production costs and to improve market acceptance represents another part of the challenge and joy for me in Fashion Design.

I look forward to an interview with you, Ms. Fried, in which we can discuss my possible contributions to Gypsy G. I will look forward to your call at your earliest convenience to arrange for an interview.

Thank you.

                        Sincerely,

                        Casey Fleur

CHAPTER 5

Street Maps and Mind Maps Sold Here

Pre-Interview Preparation

Great! Your cover letter and resume got you an interview! Now what?

I'm a "directions" person. I like road maps, atlases, globes. Before I go on an interview in a town or city that's not familiar to me, I get a map of the place and study it a few times. I have, on occasion, made a "dry run" in my car to see exactly how long it would take to get to the interview with at least ten minutes to spare. So when anyone asks me,"What do I do before the interview to get ready?" I say, *"Rehearse the route and get there early."*

On the actual day of your interview, depart a half hour earlier than the time it takes, so that even if you encounter construction, a detour, a traffic accident, a slow-moving farm vehicle on a two-lane road, or a sudden blizzard, you will arrive in plenty of time.

Having arrived early (with fifteen or twenty minutes to spare), *you have time for "easing into" the situation.* Step into the restroom and give your clothes and hair a final check. As you walk through the hallways, observe the tempo as employees go about their daily activities.

You should have time, after introducing yourself to the receptionist, to sit and observe the activity further. You may learn indirectly a little more about how busy the organization is, how much pressure you might be under, even what projects are ongoing.

Keep in mind, though, that secretaries and receptionists are *observers* whose opinions are respected by their employers. In a sense, *a receptionist evaluates you*, and you don't want to discuss professional and personal experiences that he or she might bring to the attention of the employer. In other words, *remember that the interview begins the minute you come in to the reception area: non-verbal behavior and casual remarks should be polite but neutral.*

Your arrival at this interview not only proves you can read street directions; it also indicates that you have a *direction for your life.* Your self-assessment of personal and professional strengths and your foresight into your professional future are the most important lines on your map.

So here's the real advance work. After you get the call that you are to be interviewed, *you should learn as much as possible about the company, school, or organization as you can.* Find out about their goals, products, range of services offered, volume of business and/or clients. *Ask yourself how all that information fits in with your goals and your lifestyle.* You will be asked that question, indirectly, in several different ways during the interview. Be able to articulate your strongest abilities to the interviewer, as well as the areas where you desire to improve. Professional employers are interested in employees who have good skills but who also wish to learn and grow. *Your self-assessment is the process that makes you employable; it is the vehicle that gets you comfortably through the job interview.* It's not too early to begin that process of reflection, even if you don't have an interview in the near future. Self-analysis of potential goals takes years of thinking and interacting with your environment (it's never actually finished!).

While defining your talents and goals and interacting with your environment, *don't ignore the larger environment either*—that of the political, economic, and social sphere in which we exist. Your creativity and viewpoint in any profession is enhanced by your knowledge of current affairs and literature in your field AND outside of it. You should be a *regular newspaper reader:* not only will you learn about the companies and organizations in your community, you will also learn about the far-ranging issues that make them tick. If you're interviewing for a teacher's position, and you understand school budgets, geography, and the latest developments in the space program on Capitol Hill, you can have better ideas for teaching. If you're interviewing for a Commercial Illustrator's position, and you know what other artists have drawn, what political themes are popular, and which ideas trigger certain emotions, you can have better ideas for designing a T-Shirt. If you're interviewing for a Retail Management position, and you understand people's motivations for buying, the amount of leisure time they have, and the way they react to the latest military crisis, you'll have the best ideas for selling.

The well-prepared interviewee, then, is a person with a sense of direction. Getting there physically is important, of course. But getting there psychologically, and knowing how to describe that place you're "at," is what makes you truly outstanding in your interview.

Hints to Remember

- Rehearse the physical route
- Rehearse your ideas
- Plan to arrive early so as to "ease into" the situation
- Arrive with a clear idea of your abilities and goals
- Keep your viewpoints current by daily reading in your field and newspapers

PART TWO

The Type of Person Who Gets the Job:

The Empowered Interviewee

CHAPTER 6

A Little Bit of an "Edge"

Nerves

Nerves. We've all got them. Under our skin, millions of tiny antennae keep us alert and warn us to stay away from drivers who weave into our lane, wind chill factors of 25 below, hot stovetops, bees, and job interviews. To most of us at some time or another, the Job interview seems a crime against nature. Our heads say we must go; our bodies say we cannot.

Yes, there will be nervousness. The wise interviewee admits that and mobilizes in order to channel it. Dr. Susan Reilly, a Personnel Research Psychologist with the U.S. Government, insists that interviewers expect you to be anxious; to have a little bit of an "edge." Think about it. Would you hire the applicant whose manner is flat and dull, even if you were looking for someone who is very relaxed?[1] Stated another way by Crome Dollase, a retired Vice-President of Mutual of New York, if you're not nervous at all, the job interviewer will think you're (a) not interested in the job, or (b) you're too cocky or self-confident to be hired for a situation where you should in fact be willing to get along with others, learn and grow.[2] Actually, as the interviewee, you should strike a happy medium: *you should be calm enough to articulate your strengths, but not so "laid back" that you appear smug.*

How do you reach that happy medium? First of all, *admit you will be nervous*. If you keep telling yourself you won't be, two things are going to happen. First, repeating that message over and over again will further acknowledge that the nervousness exists and that it's negative and damaging. Your nervousness is only amplified then. Secondly, if you keep telling yourself you won't be nervous, you won't think of any strategies to overcome your stress.

---

1. Gast, Ilene, for Dr. Susan Reilly. Telephone interview with Author, March 17, 1991.
2. Dollase, Crome. Telephone Interview with Author, March 28, 1991.

Having taken the first step by admitting that you will be nervous, you can start to deal with it, and dealing with it has everything to do with your pre-interview preparation. As stated in Chapter Five, you must enter the interview door with knowledge of yourself, your goals, and the organization that interviews you. Simply put, *knowledge reduces stress.*[3] If you know enough about the company and your skills to enable you to see where you can fit in, then you've taken care of much of your nervousness before the interview. Knowing how you can help the interviewer's organization gives you a healthy perspective on the interview. You should remember that the interviewer, after all, is just as hopeful as you are. "Realize that the casting director—the interviewer—needs you and wants you to do well," says Carol Nadell, president of Selective Casting in New York City.[4]

Of course, it's possible that you've engaged in a lengthy self-analysis and you know you can do this job. But you're STILL nervous. If it's our fear of failure, then, that's making you nervous, it's time for *a little pep talk* in which you reinforce your strengths and skills.[5] You could also *rehearse your interview.* Reilly suggests rehearsing with someone who doesn't know what you'll be doing in this prospective job, so that you can test how well you articulate your abilities.

Don't spend ALL your pre-interview time in rehearsal, though. Spend some time talking to the friends who are best at boosting your ego. Reilly suggests you stay away from the people who lower your self-esteem. Plan a reward AFTER the interview too: lunch with a friend, some window-shopping time, etc. Anticipation of a pleasant activity on the same day of the interview can supersede some of the discomforting thoughts you're having. Also, if you can help it, *never schedule two interviews in one day—it's too nerve-wracking.*

All of these strategies can alleviate your stress and make you feel that you're in control before and during the interview. What happens, though, if you've done all you can, you've made it halfway through the interview, and your nerves take over anyway? Suddenly you draw a mental blank, or you fear you're not explaining something as articulately as you had wanted to. Having conducted hundreds of interviews for management positions, Dollase offers an interesting suggestion. *You can pause; you CAN honestly admit your nervousness.* You can say, "I'm sorry. I'm nervous." You can even tell them why: "The real reason I'm nervous is because this is important to me and I'm excited about it. This position seems to be a real match between my skills and your needs here, and I want to explain how in

---

3. Gast, Ilene, for Dr. Susan Reilly. Telephone Interview with Author, March 17, 1991.
4. Furse, Jane, "Playing the Part," *Job Hunting Guide, Executive Female,* May–June, 1989, p. 25.
5. Dollase, Crome. Telephone Interview with Author, March 28, 1991.

the best way I can." Few interviewers would come down hard on someone who is sincere.[6]

Take care of the physical details that can take the edge off your stress as well. *Don't opt for uncomfortable clothing even though you want to look your best.* For instance, don't wear new shoes that are too tight. Choose your "interview" clothes carefully, but choose something you really ENJOY wearing. Nothing is a more apt metaphor for an awkward interview than shoes that don't fit and clothes that feel strange. Also, as stated in Chapter Five, do yourself a favor by *arriving early* to give yourself some "easing-in" time.

If you follow all of these strategies and hints, and you STILL feel that you and the interviewer didn't connect, then *disconnect yourself.* You must separate yourself from the experience by refusing to take it personally. Reilly advises you above all not to blame yourself. If the interviewer puts you through a rough session, the chances are good that he or she is doing that to everyone. It's not your fault.

How could it be? You know what to do for an interview! Now, let's talk more about what to wear.

Hints to Remember

- Knowledge reduces stress: Study the company so that you know what you can do for them.
- Rehearse your ideas with someone who doesn't know much about the position.
- See people who boost your self-esteem before the interview.
- Admit sincerely that you're nervous if you have difficulty during the interview.
- Wear comfortable clothing that won't add to physical stress.

---

6. Dollase Interview.

CHAPTER 7

You Are What You Wear

What to Wear

The person who gets hired is the person who gives the best first impression. Sounds trite and maybe a little unfair, but think for a minute or four. It usually takes anywhere up to four minutes for a stranger, your interviewer, to not only make a first impression, assessment or judgement, but to also determine whether or not you will remain strangers or build an employer/employee relationship. "Why four minutes? It is not an arbitrary interval. Rather, it is the average time, demonstrated by careful observation, during which strangers in a social situation interact before they decide to part or continue their encounter."[1] Therefore, what you wear to your interview is crucial, because, like it or not, you're going to give a lasting impression.

Before we get into the wardrobe issue, *general hygiene* cannot be overlooked. Take time out for your nails and hair; a simple manicure can do wonders for the most neglected nails. You'll be speaking with your hands to some degree, so you can't hide them. If you bite your nails, you might want to stop for a few days, if possible, before the interview. If needed, there are a number of products on the market now that can help you with this, temporarily or permanently. While we are on the subject of hands, do you have discoloration due to smoking, or because of certain things you do with your hands, such as painting or tinkering under the hood of your car? Again, get a product that will help diminish, if not eliminate those stains.

Scrutinize your outer shell objectively, if not critically, keeping in mind you may not get a second chance. Apply *makeup* lightly on the day of your interview, to avoid distracting yourself from yourself. Lipstick that is too bright, or too much eye shadow will distract your interviewer; think

---

1. Zunin, M.D., Leonard with Natalie Zunin. *Contact: The First Four Minutes* (New York: Ballantine Books), 1972.

38 PART TWO: The Empowered Interviewee

natural looking. The same is true for your *hair style.* You want it to enhance your looks, not take away from it!

Now, for the *clothes* you'll wear. *The best place to look is in your closet.* Don't feel compelled to go out and buy something new. That will drive you crazy and broke. You usually don't know what to expect to wear; therefore, *think conservatively.* Once you get inside where you might be working, you can see for yourself what the employees are wearing. When you have successfully landed a job, and have received a paycheck or two, then you can shop for some clothes that suit you and your new working environment. Wait, though, for you may find people may be more casual or more formal than you originally thought.

Before the day of the interview, however, plan and put an outfit or two together. No matter what time of year it is, you're *safe with neutral colors.* Stay away from something too bright or flashy. This is not the time to make a fashion statement. Look for the classic looking suit that has worked for uncertain situations before. Or pull together something that coordinates well. For example, your basic black skirt (or trousers for men) and a plaid jacket/sportjacket.

A sure bet for women, besides a simple suit, is a skirt or dress with hemlines that reveal style know-how without extremes. *Don't go too short or too long.* The point is you want to complement your positive attributes.

Your *accessories* should be the finishing touches, not the main attraction. *Keep them simple.* Nothing dangling, bangling, or banging. You might want to take rings off to insure your privacy. Bracelets on your writing wrist may make it awkward for you to take notes. Wristwatches are a must, but no Mickey Mouse or Swatch watches. Shoes should aid in your walking, not hinder it, so keep heels low. You might not bother with a purse, so there won't be the tendency to forget it or have it in the way for a handshake. Keep your wallet, keys, and other personal items in your briefcase, if you elect not to carry a purse. If you opt for a purse, keep it in your lap so you don't forget it. A final word, ladies: pants are both 'in' and here to stay, but they're not for the job interview.

And, yes gentlemen, *you do have to wear a tie.* Your suit doesn't have to be a two piece or a three piece, but your slacks and jacket should coordinate. Reach for the khaki or gray flannel pants, topped with a navy blue blazer, if you have them. A white or light colored shirt and subtle tie will do quite nicely. The same holds true for males as for females in the accessory line: keep it simple! The gold chain (and earring) should stay home. Everyone should *watch the cologne or the perfume:* little or none goes a long way, or lot longer than too much.

You may want to *try on what you think you'd like to wear to the interview a day or two in advance,* in case something needs a stitch or button. You'll want to give it a fresh press if it's wrinkled or creased. You'll look fine if you follow these very basic rules, and you'll feel even better if you plan ahead, tell yourself you look great, and SMILE.

Hint to Remember

- Project a neat and clean appearance and dress conservatively.

CHAPTER 8

How You Say "I Want the Job"

Empowerment

Here at Cazenovia College, we require our students to be interviewees in a mock job interview as part of our "Effective Speaking" course.[1] The project is part of Effective Speaking because the job interview involves communication at its most practical. What could be a more practical aspect of the interview process than knowing how to say you want the job? This is the idea of *empowerment*.

You must be assertive, but you can't be insistent. You must be eager, but you can't beg. You must remember that even if you don't come right out and say, "I want the job," you get the message across not only by what you say, but by the way you say it.

First, remember that written communication is as important as oral communication. Your cover letter starts this process.[2] Then, a note to confirm your appointment with the interviewer (once the appointment has been made) should be sent. This is an opportunity to state your interest and to help you stand out among the other interviewees.[3] It's a brief note, written in business-letter form, where you should simply state that you are pleased that you will be meeting with Mrs. Jones on Tuesday at 3:30 and that you are looking forward to the interview. You should also send a thank-you note after the interview (again in business-letter form) stating that you enjoyed talking with Mrs. Jones and hope to hear from her soon. Neither form of communication would be regarded as "pesty;" both would clearly demonstrate your interest as well as your thoughtfulness.

Crome Dollase, a retired Vice President of Mutual of New York, suggests a *four-part approach to establishing your interest* during the

---

1. For hints on the Mock Job Interview, See Chapter 23.
2. For hints on the Cover Letter, see Chapter 4.
3. Dollase, Crome. Telephone Interview with Author, March 28, 1991.

interview process itself. First, *verify that the interviewer still has your resume* or that he/she has the correct one. In a large firm where several interviews take place in one day, this might not always be the case. Second, *think of the position as a "match" for your skills and state it as such.* Toward the end of the interview, you can say something like, "I'm excited about what I've learned from you today. I think I've got the match that you need here." Third, *ask good questions* that show that you're planning to invest your future in the firm. Ask about benefits, training and in-service programs that can enhance your skills, opportunities for advancement. And last, *leave SOMETHING with the interviewer at the end:* a portfolio, an expanded resume, or a publicity piece about one of your relevant accomplishments.[4]

Another way of showing your seriousness about the job is to ask, near the end of the interview, "What is your time frame for filling this position? I'd like to know what your decision will be." After the interviewer tells you when he/she will be making a decision, it's all right to ask if you may call the office to find out what that decision is.

With these various approaches, you show your interviewer that you can take the lead in seeking out what is best for yourself, calmly but definitely. Your sincere questions and your concern for your future growth become expressions of empowerment that then can leave the interviewer with a memorable impression.

Hints to Remember

- You need to send two notes that demonstrate interest: a confirmation of your appointment before the interview and a thank-you note after the interview.
- The key word is "match." Remind the interviewer that you can match your skills with the position's responsibilities.
- Ask questions that show your interest in a future with the company.
- Ask when a decision will be made.
- Leave the interviewer some extra material about your accomplishments.

---

4. Dollase Interview.

CHAPTER 9

Telling the Truth

The final part of preparation: thinking about the *quality* of the answers you're about to give.

There is only one rule to remember about telling the truth:

TELL THE BEST TRUTH YOU HAVE, BUT ALWAYS TELL THE TRUTH.

Or, to put another way, try to put the best face on the truth, but don't try to deny, avoid or change the truth.

> "No, I have no real experience in this field, but that means that I come in with no preconceptions about how to do the job and you can train me to do it your way."

> "Yes, I was fired for (chronic lateness/chronic absenteeism/stealing/lying/cursing out a customer), but I was young and immature and I learned my lesson and I know better now."

If you choose to answer an illegal question (and, as we will note in Chapter 14, the choice is *yours*), answer it truthfully, but answer it *only in the present tense.*

> "No, we're not planning any children" (Don't include the qualifying "now" or "in the immediate future.")

Hint to Remember

- *TELL THE BEST TRUTH YOU HAVE, BUT ALWAYS TELL THE TRUTH.*

PART THREE

The Heart of the Matter:

The Questions, and How You Answer Them

CHAPTER 10

You Never Get a Second Chance to Make a First Impression

That First One Minute

Henry Rogers, chairman of the Rogers and Cowan Public relations firm, tells this story of interviewing a young man:

> "I walked over to him, shook his weak, clammy hand, and sat down... 'Our mutual friend, Mr. Fischer, tells me that you're interested in getting into the public-relations business.' 'Yes, I am,' came the response. I waited for him to continue. He didn't. I picked up the conversation. 'Why does it interest you?' 'Well, I guess I like people and I get along with people very well.' I groaned inwardly... 'What do you know about public relations?' 'Not very much,' he admitted. I tried to catch his eye, but I couldn't. He was looking at my left shoe."[1]

In the first one minute, that young man made five critical blunders, all of which irritated the interviewer. Needless to say, he was not hired. Research shows that most employers decide a job applicant's fate in the first thirty seconds of an interview. So it's critically important to make a good first impression.

Greet interviewers with a firm, sweat-free handshake. Remember, it's just a handshake; don't get into an arm wrestling match, because you lose points for breaking bones. Furthermore, it's best to let interviewers initiate the handshake. If they don't extend a hand, it would be improper for you to shove your hand into their face. Instead of seeming polite, you'll appear overly aggressive and intrusive.

Be personable. *Your resume and cover letter get you the interview, but your personality often wins the job.* Be warm, enthusiastic, and confident.

---

1. Henry C. Rogers, *Rogers' Rules for Success* (New York: St. Martin's/Marek, 1984), pp. 73–74.

47

48 PART THREE: The Questions and How You Answer Them

As mentioned in Chapter Six, you must control your *nerves*. If you find yourself chewing gum or smoking a cigarette on your way to the interview, be sure the gum and the smoky breath are gone before you walk into the office. Don't get flustered if the applicant interviewed before you looks older and wiser, or if you're kept waiting while the interviewer takes a phone call, or if you discover that you're going to be interviewed by an entire panel of people, or if the interviewer starts taking notes. Try to adapt to any unexpected occurrences.

Psychologists advise that if you're given the choice of sitting in a chair in front or beside the interviewer's desk, *choose the one beside the desk*. As noted by Dr. Joyce Brothers, "this way, there are no barriers between the two of you, so you automatically become a little more equal, and the interviewer unconsciously respects you a little more."[2] Of course, you should sit up straight in the chair; there is a big difference between looking relaxed and slouching.

It's important to have good eye contact with the interviewer immediately, because it shows them that you are interested in what they are saying. In addition, if you maintain eye contact when you talk, you appear honest and sincere. This does not mean you should get into a staring contest with the interviewer; maintain natural eye contact.

Every question has significance in an interview, even the seemingly innocent ones that usually break the ice, so stay on guard. If the interviewer asks, "This building can be very confusing. Did you have a hard time finding our office?" and you admit that you barely made the interview on time, the interviewer will think that you are not a good problem solver. If the interviewer asks, "Don't you just hate rainy days like this?" and you say, "Yeah. I never even want to get out of bed when it rains this hard," the interviewer may think you'd only show up for work on sunny days.

If the interviewer begins by saying, "So, you want an accounting career?" don't just say, "Yes." If you're asked, "Why does this field interest you?" don't say "I like it." Brief replies like that make the interviewer think you have a limited vocabulary. Similarly, if the interviewer asks, "Why do you think you can do this job?" don't stop after saying "I had good grades in these courses in school." Questions like that provide great opportunities for you to go on the offensive, discuss your strengths, and guide the path of the conversation. Plan your responses in advance, so you can hit cream puff questions like that out of the park for a home run, and immediately show the interviewer how well you can communicate.

---

2. Dr. Joyce Brothers, "How to Get the Job You Want," *Parade*, November 16, 1986, p. 5.

A lot of things can go wrong during that first minute, but if you're well-prepared and confident, you can make that critical first impression a good one. You probably won't get a second chance.

Hints to Remember

- Your personality *can* win you a job.
- Greet the interviewer with a smile and a firm, dry handshake.
- Maintain good Eye Contact.
- Answer questions carefully and confidently.

CHAPTER 11

Turnabout, Fair Play:

What the Interviewer is Thinking

'Walk a mile in another person's shoes.' This is one cliche that offers excellent advice, particularly in a job interview. It is impossible to do well in any situation which involves your being judged, if you don't think about the demands and the character of the judge.

First, some general thoughts on the person behind that desk.

1. The Interviewer does not want to hire someone that he or she will only have to fire in a few months.

Most interviewers are not the person who will ultimately be responsible for overseeing you on the job. If *you* fail, then *they* fail—they've cost the company money and the ever-more valuable commodity of time, and they have embarrassed themselves professionally. As a result....

2. The interviewer's job security may well hinge on their ability to perform the above task.

3. As a result of 1 and 2 above, it makes no sense for the interviewer to try to "trick" or "destroy" the candidate. If they make mincemeat out of you, they'll never get the information that they need to see if you can do the job.

4. Most interviewers do this so often—sometimes many times in one day, that they get bored easily.

All the answers are the same—that's because all the *questions* are essentially the same.

51

5. Despite the above, the interviewer does not see it to be his or her job to keep the interview from becoming boring.

That, quite plainly, is the candidate's job. And too many ill-prepared candidates seem to expect that, for whatever reason, the *interviewer* will bail them out.

6. There are, of course, good and bad interviewers.

If you're in the market for more than two interviews, you'll meet them both.

7. A bad interviewer will simply ask you questions.

You'll *feel* the list that they have written down on their clipboard. They may even *number* their questions for you ("My first question . . ." My next question . . ." "In conclusion . . ."). Either that, or they'll just have your *resume* in front of them, and they will wing the interview from that piece of paper (guaranteed, they haven't read it ahead of time, and before the interview is done, they'll get your name wrong at least once). A poor interviewer finds out nothing about the candidate, so they make an uninformed decision; you found out nothing about the company, except that they employ people who can't interview.

8. A truly good interviewer understands that the answer to the question isn't nearly as important as *how* the candidate answers the questions.

This is the key point that anyone teaching someone how to be an interviewer (yes, it is a teachable skill—there are as many texts and guides for *them* as there are for *you*, and many colleges have courses just for this purpose) wants to get across. It makes sense to try to list some of the thoughts going through the mind of a good interviewer, as you try to answer the question that students have been asking about teachers for centuries: "What Do They *Want*?"

a. The good interviewer has already read your resume, and they have already decided that you have the qualifications that they need for that particular job.

b. Now, what they need to find out is if you can *do* the job.

Good interviewers don't plan out a list of questions. They think about the type of person that they need to hire, and they plan the interview around those needs.

Take, for example, a person who is interviewing to hire a day-care instructor. Patience is high on their list of "needs" in a potential employee. A poor interviewer will look at you and ask the dumbest question in the world: "Do you consider yourself to be a patient person?" (Like you're going to say "no"). A good interviewer will design questions to see if you are, indeed, a patient person (for whatever it's worth, one great way to do this is to repeat the same question a number of times, just to see if the candidate blows up). A poorly prepared interviewee sees these as "trick questions." A candidate who knows what the interviewer needs to learn from the candidate sees this as the most logical and effective strategy for a job interview.

    c.   Therefore, a good interviewer will converse with you.

They will probe a bit; ask follow-up questions, ask interesting questions. They will watch you, taking notes less on what you say than on the way you say it (notes like, "they don't seem sincere;" "He really looks like he cares," "He's lying to me!" are commonplace on an interviewer's legal pad). This is all carefully designed by the interviewer to find out who you are. Their questions will be a means toward this end, designed less to get specific information on your qualifications (most of that is on the resume), but to help them paint a full picture of you.

One hint that may help put this idea into some perspective. I tell my students in interviewing tactics to treat the candidate as a prospective office mate. Will you feel comfortable leaving money on your desk unattended if this person is in your office? Will you enjoy their company? Will they work hard, and not leave you in the lurch? Will they lie to you? Can they do the job, and be enjoyable to be around? That's what a good interviewer is looking for.

One final point. All of the above should destroy the nonsensical myth, propagated by too many interviewing guides and texts, that the interviewer is some sort of adversary who needs to be 'conquered' by the candidate in order for them to get the job. Not only does that make no logical sense—after all, why try to dominate a person who will decide on your fate—neither does it make any strategic sense. If the interviewer is judging you on how good a work partner you'll be, then act like you'll make a good work partner! *Talk* to them, don't try to *beat* them.

Hints to Remember

- It is to the interviewer's advantage to run a fair interview that finds out as much about you as possible.

- A good interviewer is more concerned with *how* you answer his or her questions than with the answer itself.

- A good interviewer is not checking your qualifications; rather, they are gauging whether or not you are the type of person who can do that job.

CHAPTER 12

This is Not a Multiple Choice Exam . . .
How to Respond to *Any* Question

If you read the previous chapter carefully, you won't be surprised when you do not find the traditional "List of Twenty Questions Found in any Job Interview, and Some Suggested Answers" in this book. To me, that's as close to useless as it gets. In our next chapter, you'll be reading about strategies for tricky questions, not prepared answers. The interviewee is trying to find out about YOU—the whole person. You prepare yourself for—indeed, you guarantee a bad interview, if all you do to prepare yourself for the question is to think about the answers.

This is, to me, the biggest problem in preparing a candidate for a job interview. They try to predict questions, and memorize the perfect reply. No one, particularly an interviewer who has just been through ten boring interviews with people with pat answers—wants to talk to a robot. If you accept the fact that the interviewer has already judged most of your qualifications from your resume, and is now interviewing you to find out if you are the right person for the job, you shoot yourself in the foot if you try to second-guess them. You'll sound cocky. *Don't memorize questions. Don't memorize answers. In fact, don't memorize* anything.

Instead, try the following to prepare yourself for the questions: *make out a list of "needs" for the position*—just like the good interviewer has done. Day Care Instructor? Patience; even-tempered, quick to take charge in an emergency; creative; caring, to name but a few. This should be easy —if you don't have most of these characteristics, you probably won't enjoy the training enough to get to the interview stage! Then, *try to answer the questions in a manner that highlights these qualities.* Don't try to predict questions—just sound, look, and act like the type of person who will fit that job.

55

With that in mind, here are five hints to help you while you are actually answering their question:

1. Be enthusiastic.

Smile if you can. Sound like you want the job. If you don't care, the only thing that the interviewer will learn about you is that you don't care. No matter how good your qualifications are on paper, no interviewer—unless they're a fool—will hire you if you don't sound like you want to do the job.

2. Nothing is more important than Point Number One. But . . .

3. Avoid one-word responses.

Chat. Keep it conversational.

4. Avoid language that makes you look childish or incapable of handling a mature position.

"Yup." "Nope." "Yeah." "I guess so." "Uh, huh."

5. Watch the interviewer.

Keeping good eye contact does not mean staring at them for an hour. You won't lose out if you break eye concentration for a moment. But good listening involves watching the person you're talking to—you can get a feel for what they really want to know by reading their eyes and their body language—just like a good interviewer is doing to you.

For you to be successful, the interviewer needs to learn that you are the type of person that they can work with, and the type of professional who can do the job. That's an attitude; a personae. There's no amount of studying, or memorizing of lists, that can prep you to do well in that department.

Hints to Remember

- Don't memorize either questions or answers.
- Remember that you are there to show that you have the qualities that the interviewer needs in an employee—keep those qualities in mind as you answer *any* question.

CHAPTER 13

Now, Tell Me About Yourself...

Strategies for Often-Asked Questions

The most important thing you can do to prepare to answer an interviewer's questions is just that—*prepare*. As exciting as it is to a receive a call from a prospective employer, remember that getting an interview is a far cry from getting a job. As soon as you know that you hang up the phone, begin to prepare. As we have discussed in Chapter Five, preparation should include research: find out as much as you can about the company, the interviewer and the job itself. But most importantly, plan for that all important thirty minute ordeal—the interview itself. Anticipate the questions, plan your responses, and rehearse those responses. If possible, have a friend ask you these questions and *tape record your responses to them*. When you listen to your answers, ask yourself (honestly) if you would hire yourself. If the answer is "No," there still will be time to refine and polish your answers. Remember that you are only one of a number of candidates who are being interviewed for the position—you must prove to the interviewer that you are the best of the lot. Each question the interviewer asks is an opportunity you have to prove that.

Most questions will fall into one of three categories: *educational background, work experience and personal background*. Go over your resume, looking for areas which might be perceived as liabilities, and consider how questions about those areas can be transformed into assets. Review the job description, and identify the aspects of the job which correspond to your educational, experiential or personal strengths.

During the interview itself, the most important thing you can do is to *listen* carefully to the questions you are asked. Here are some questions that will probably appear, in some form or other, during the course of almost every interview:

1. Why are you interested in this job?

This one should be easy. Since you've thoroughly researched the company, you *know* why you want to work there. Be specific about the aspects of the company that appeal to you: "You make the best widgets on the market." Mention names of people you've talked to: "My neighbor, Mr. Jones, deals with your company. He's told me about your innovative management structure." At all costs, avoid "I just needed a job, so I applied everywhere I could think of."

2. What is your greatest strength?

This question is an incredible opportunity. Now you can show how well suited you are to the company. Be sure the strength you choose is work related! Reliability, loyalty, a willingness to work hard—any of these will be on an employer's checklist.

3. What is your greatest weakness?

Turn this one to your advantage. Never mention a characteristic that will give the employer a reason to turn you down. Turn this question to your advantage by showing traits which will show your commitment to hard work, reliability, etc. Something like "I've been told my standards are too high," or "I'm overly sensitive to details," can work here. Nobody's perfect, and your employer doesn't expect you to be. Your answer here indicates your honesty as well as your perception of yourself. Really think through your response to this question.

4. What would you like to be doing five years from now?

This can be a tricky question. The interviewer is trying to find out both your commitment to the company and your ambition. Think about the things that could be achieved by the ideal candidate in the position. Frequently people reveal in their answer to this question what they would *really* like to be doing. Sound ambitious, but not as if this job is a mere stepping stone.

5. Why did you leave your last job?

Be honest, but *never* badmouth your previous employer. If you feel that your job is a dead end, and you lack room for advancement, or it has become routine, say so. Don't mention salary, personalities, or benefits here.

6. Why are you interested in this company?

Here, too, your research pays off. Be specific about the aspects of the company which you find most appealing. Show how your strengths as an employee match the needs of the company. Be enthusiastic and informed.

7. Tell me about yourself.

This is a JOB INTERVIEW. Your answer to this question, while it can be informally expressed, should be JOB RELATED!

Remember that for most employers, attitude and the ability to speak well are the most important traits employers look for in a candidate. The job interview is the only place the employer can judge those qualities. If you prepare for it seriously and thoroughly, you'll have a strong advantage over your competition.

Hints to Remember

- Honestly assess your *job related* strengths and weaknesses.
- Remember the research you've done—your answers to questions should be those of the ideal candidate for *that company*.
- Rehearse, but don't memorize.

CHAPTER 14

Know Before You Go!

Controlling Illegal Questions

You may be intentionally or unintentionally asked unfair questions in your job interview. This may happen even though federal law prohibits questions which discriminate on the basis of such factors as "sex, age, race, national origin, color of skin, religion, marital status or disability."[1]

It's not easy to delineate all these questions, since each state has their own list of lawful and unlawful questions. You can contact your state's Fair Employment Practices Commission or the State Division of Human Rights for a more extensive list.[2]

You must listen carefully to distinguish between a fair and an unfair question. The test of fairness is always *job relevancy*. You must decide whether or not a question is pertinent to the position. Listen to the close nuances of meaning between these lawful and unlawful questions listed by New York State:[3]

Lawful	*Unlawful*
1. Are you a citizen *of the U.S.?*	1. *Of what country* are you a citizen?
2. Do you speak *fluent Spanish?*	2. What is your native *language?*
3. Have you served in the *Air Force?*	3. Have you served in the *military?*

As a recent graduate, you may want, or *need*, this job. How will *you* answer these questions so that you aren't eliminated from the job search?

You must form some tactful answers. For example, perhaps the interviewer asks the illegal question, "Have you been arrested?" If you can

---

1. Gary T. Hunt and William F. Eadie, *Interviewing* (New York: Holt, Rinehart and Winston, 1987), p. 187.
2. Anthony Medley, *Sweaty Palms: The Neglected Art of Being Interviewed* (Berkeley, CA, Ten Speed Press, 1984), p. 165.
3. *Sweaty Palms*, p. 169.

61

answer the question *without harming your job chances,* you might say, "No, I've never been arrested, but didn't I read somewhere that that's not an appropriate question to ask in an interview?" This lets them know that you are aware of the law on employment practices, but you *must* keep a pleasant tone, so as not to offend your interviewer.[4]

If the interviewer *persists* in asking these questions, you'll sound threatening if you say, "I can't answer that because it's an illegal question, and those are against the law!" It is better to sound as if the interviewer is *teasing you,* and respond lightly: "You don't really want me to answer that, do you?" This lets you decline an answer and signals the employer that this question shouldn't be asked.[5]

If your interviewer deliberately continues to ask discriminatory questions, or in some way sexually harasses you, you can file charges with the Equal Opportunity Commission. The charges must be filed within 180 days of the interview.[6] Unfortunately, unfair interviewing practices are difficult to prove in court, since the burden of proof is on *you* to show discrimination.

The issue of fair questions and fair employment tests are still somewhat blurry. As noted in Chapter Eleven, interviewers are sometimes inexperienced and ask awkward questions *unintentionally.* If you file a claim, be sure that you were *intentionally* discriminated against, and be ready to prove it.[7]

Hints to Remember

- Prepare by thinking ahead how you will answer an unfair question.
- Listen carefully to the question and ask the interviewer for clarification or relevancy.
- Take time to form a tactful answer.
- Keep good eye contact and present yourself positively.

---

4. *Sweaty Palms,* p. 171.
5. *Sweaty Palms,* p. 171.
6. *Sweaty Palms,* p. 172.
7. Hunt and Eadie, *Interviewing,* p. 188.

CHAPTER 15

"Uh, Excuse Me . . . But About the Money?"

The Question of Salary

Well, here you are, after all this . . . finally interviewing with a great company. All signs indicate that the interviewer is going to offer you the job. Dreams of financial independence begin to form, while visions of payday dance in your head.

Payday . . . You suddenly realize that money has not been mentioned. What does this job pay, anyway? *DON'T ASK!* Because, although there may not be such a thing as a stupid question, there certainly is such a thing as an impolitic one. *The etiquette of interviewing dictates that the interviewer raises the salary issue and the interviewee does not.* You are expected to politely foster the fiction that you would consider it an honor to work for this company for free (Of course they know better, but it pleases them to think you are more concerned with responsibilities than with compensation).

Once the interviewer introduces the salary issue, however, you must be prepared to manage the negotiations to your best advantage. Salary is much too important to be an afterthought. Your standard of living may well be affected by how skillfully you handle this discussion.

Once again, preparation is key to your interviewing success. Before your interview:

1. Determine the salary you need in order to meet your financial goals.

Prepare your own budget, then look for job offers that have the potential of meeting your financial needs.

2. Ask specifically what job you will be interviewing for when you are called to an interview.

63

The more you know before you go in, the more you can research.

3. Research the salary range for the type of job for which you are interviewing.

Ask people who are employed in the field and anyone you may know who works for the company. This information will help you to realistically answer a question about your salary expectations that the interviewer may ask. Frequently, there is a salary range for any given job and where you fall in that range will be determined in part by the experience, education, and skills you bring to the job. In addition to salary, other benefits like insurance, vacation time, pension plan, and company stock plan make up what is called the compensation package. Although there may be room for some negotiation on salary, usually the remainder of the package is non-negotiable.

So, let's get back to a well-prepared you in the middle of that interview. You wait patiently for the interviewer to raise the salary issue. Ideally, the interviewer has decided you are the right person for the job. He or she informs you that the salary for the job is $X amount and that, if that is satisfactory, the hiring process can be set in motion. You know from your research that the salary is fair, considering your experience and in light of the salaries paid to others for similar work. It is also a salary on which you can manage your finances. You accept the offer graciously (no outbursts of exuberance, please) and you've got a done deal.

The salary discussion may be just that simple. The employer knows that you will be a better employee if you are paid a fair wage for your work. He or she also knows that if you are not compensated adequately, you may soon move on to another job and the employer will then have to go through another costly hiring and training period for your replacement. Fair compensation is just plain good business.

Not all salary resolutions are ideal, however. Let's look at a few variations on theme:

1. The interviewer asks, *"What kind of salary expectations do you have?"*

This is a question that allows you to show you've done your homework. You say, "I understand the range for this type of work is from $X to $Z. With my three years of experience in the field, I would expect to be near the top of that range." Another approach to take, if asked to name a salary, is to say, "I'd rather look at salary in light of the total compensation package, rather than to name a set figure. Would you tell me about the compensation program and the salary range?"

2. The interviewer asks, *"What salary are you currently earning?"*

First and foremost, *DO NOT MISREPRESENT THE FACTS!* If your present salary is substantially lower than the range for the job for which you are interviewing—and if there is a good reason for that lower salary—you might counter with, "Let me preface my answer by saying that one of the reasons I am looking for a new position is that my compensation at my present job is far below what I can be earning with my education and my experience." Your present job may be in the not-for-profit arena, which traditionally pays on a lower scale than the commercial sphere. Or perhaps your present employer is a small company that is unable to pay competitive wages. If your case allows for an explanation, keep it short and directly related to the point.

Unless you are truly willing to walk away from the job offer, *DON'T BE INFLEXIBLE ABOUT SALARY.* By stating you couldn't possibly accept a penny lower than $X, you may be shutting down negotiations prematurely. If the salary quoted is lower than you feel is fair, you may say, "That is really less than I had anticipated. I would very much like to work here. Can we talk further about a somewhat higher figure in light of my qualifications?" Remember, this is a time to negotiate, not to stonewall. Should the interviewer not offer any possibility for negotiation, you may ask about the timeliness of reviews and when you might expect the opportunity to advance to a higher salary.

Whatever the case, do not go on about how you really need the money. That is not the interviewer's concern and it may well put you in a bad light. Negotiations for salary should be based on your merits, not on your needs.

EXCEPTIONS TO THE RULE: Although you should leave the introduction of the salary discussion to the interviewer, there are exceptions. *Should you reach the end of the second interview and salary has not been mentioned, then you may politely ask the salary range for the position.* Also, should you be absolutely firm on a salary below which you will not accept a job—despite whatever benefits may be offered—and if you have reason to believe that the position for which you are interviewing falls below that figure, you may ask about salary to save you and the interviewer time. This should be done with great diplomacy and tact or you may find that the interviewer assumes you are simply a greedy person who is more concerned with money than with responsibility.

Hints to Remember

- Prepare to discuss salary by researching and rehearsing.
- Don't raise the subject of salary. Wait for the interviewer to make the first move.
- Always answer honestly when asked about current salary levels.
- Don't be afraid to negotiate, if your research shows the offer is too low.
- Look at the entire compensation package before digging your heels in about salary.

CHAPTER 16

Body Talk Speaks Louder Than Words

Non-Verbal Communication

Answer this: What do people buy first, verbal or non-verbal language? If you respond verbal, you're wrong. Your listeners are always more attuned to your body talk!

In the preceding chapters you've read and learned what questions to ask and prepared to answer, what not to say, and how to answer some rather tricky questions tactfully. During your interview you will be sending off other messages with your body *that will come, for the most part, naturally.* But by being aware of your body, you'll be more influential in your non-verbal messages.

Eye contact is crucial during this encounter, as it is in most dyadic or small group settings. There is nothing more annoying than having someone not look at you while your trying to carry on a conversation. Keep your eyes on the interviewer. It will keep you more focused too, and you'll be able to respond to your interviewer's non-verbal clues as well. Don't stare however.

Your *posture* should exude confidence. When you enter the doorway and are first greeted by your interviewer, stand straight, smile, and get ready for a firm handshake. Never slouch or lean on something. When you are asked to sit, sit down gracefully and sit so you are sitting up straight with your feet on the ground, if possible. This will make it easier for you to take notes on your interview. Don't fidget, swing, or kick with your legs, feet, and hands. Lean forward in your chair and maintain a comfortable posture. Be relaxed and place your *hands* on your lap until you are ready gesture meaningfully. You'll use your hands naturally as you do whenever you talk.

Your *facial gestures* will also come naturally, but be aware of what messages you may be sending with your face. Don't act surprised by raising your eyebrows at an illegal question, for instance. Or, don't frown at your interviewer if you are confused or don't like what you're hearing.

When you sit down, don't cross your legs, except at your ankles. Men have more freedom with *their posture* this, but even so, it is best not to send a too-relaxed message by sitting too casually relaxed with crossed legs.

If you remember to smile appropriately and nod affirmatively, you'll appear positive and friendly, and you'll feel relaxed. *Probably the single most important projection you give of yourself is your attitude;* your attitude towards yourself, others around you, and what you have to offer. Use your non-verbal behavior to convey positive qualities about yourself. Make the most of your time, so remind yourself ahead of time of these behaviors and work on that positive attitude!

Hint to Remember

- "Belief . . . Confidence . . . Attitude Equals Victory."

Norman Vincent Peale

CHAPTER 17

I'm Deciding On You, Too!

"Now, Do *You* Have Any Questions?"

As noted in Chapter Eleven, a good interview is a two-way process. The company learns about you and you learn about them. Research the company and the position carefully by bringing a list of questions with you to the interview. Although you must let the interviewer direct the interview, at some point there should be an opportunity to reverse roles. Asking questions conveys interest and preparation. It's another chance to show you've done your homework! This is the time to investigate the company, management policies, job duties and future opportunities.

Interviews are the place to match your individual goals to company goals. You may wish to ask broad questions such as:

1. What are the company's future plans and goals?

2. Can you show me an organizational chart so I can see where I fit in?

3. What is the biggest single problem facing your company right now?

4. What will my career path be if I started with this position?

5. How does this company motivate or encourage top performance?

This is also the perfect time to clarify the duties for this position:

1. How many people have held this job in the last five years?

2. Why is the position vacant?

3. What would you like me to accomplish in this position?

4. How soon will the position be filled?

5. Can I feel free to call if I have more questions at a later date?

Another thing questions do for you is *relax tension*. It helps you focus on what you want to know, instead of judging your interviewing performance. *Questions let you take control and focus on the job instead of yourself.*

If you have really thought about this job and are definitely interested, several questions will occur to you. The answers to these questions will determine if you really want this position. The more information you have, the more sound your decision will be about this job.

Hints to Remember

- Research the company and the job beforehand.
- Ask questions to decide if the job fits your needs.
- Thoughtful questions show you've researched the job.
- Honest questions help you to relax because the roles reverse.

CHAPTER 18

Applying the Brakes

How to Save It When It's Going Downhill

I had an interview once with the head of personnel for a computer manufacturer. Prior to the interview, I spent days doing research on the computer field in general, and this company in particular. A computer whiz gave me a quick course in the history of computers, newspaper and magazine articles provided me with information about the company's products and the competition's ventures, and a recent employee gave me details about the company's corporate philosophy. I felt totally prepared and confident.

But the interview started off a disaster. The first thing the man said to me was, "I don't understand why you scheduled this interview; you don't seem to have any experience in the personnel area." When I explained that I was hoping to work in the training division, he shot the idea down by saying that the company had begun phasing out in-house training.

I was temporarily stunned and became unusually quiet, so the interviewer started talking at length about other areas within personnel. After I recovered, I kept trying to find a spot to join the conversation. When I finally did, his phone started ringing incessantly. The secretary had stepped out of the office, so he was forced to interrupt me and answer the call. When he was through, I began talking again, but he interrupted me when the secretary returned to tell her to hold all his calls. When I started for the third time, I got to the end of the sentence and completely blanked out on the word I was looking for. The sentence hung in midair for what seemed like forever, just waiting to be completed.

After momentarily becoming angry with myself for apparently blowing the interview I had prepared so long for, I began remembering all the things I had planned to say. When I finally began speaking coherently, I regained my confidence. I worked into the conversation things I had learned during my research, explained why I was sincerely interested in working for the company, discussed my work experience and accomplishments, and ultimately discovered that my background perfectly suited another department's needs. The interview ended with his promise that he would recommend me for employment to the head of the other department.

Obviously you would never want to start off an interview like that, but if it ever happens, don't throw in the towel. The key to turning an interview around is returning to basics—remember why you're there and remember your key strategies.

Nervousness can cause us to forget everything we wanted to accomplish, so *maintaining self-confidence is critical.* "It is fear of the unknown that attacks and weakens your resolve. But there should be no such fear in being interviewed. An interview is centered on the subject you know best: yourself."[1]

So, when things are going downhill quickly, remember that *you have the power within yourself to apply the brakes and change the course.* Another thing to remember is that *it's probably not going as badly as you think.* For example, in my interview, it felt like hours before I was able to recall the word I was thinking of, but it actually was only seconds. My interviewer might not have even thought the pause was unnatural.

Finally, remember that every interview is a learning experience. If you don't get the job, you're no worse off than when you walked in for the interview. So instead of panicking when an interview is not working out the way you wanted it to, analyze why. If you can do so while the interview is still going on, you have a good chance of turning it around. If you can't, at least learn from the experience so you don't make the same mistakes next time.

Hints to Remember

- Prepare well and communicate your selling points.
- Maintain self-confidence when things start going wrong.
- You hold the power to change your fortunes.
- Don't forget your battle plan and what you have to do to succeed.
- It's probably not going as badly as it seems.

---

1. H. Anthony Medley, *Sweaty Palms: The Neglected Art of Being Interviewed* (Berkeley, CA, Ten Speed Press, 1984), p. 98.

PART FOUR

After the Interview

CHAPTER 19

Prompt and Circumstance

Steps To Be Taken Immediately

Searching for a full time job *is* a full-time job. Think of yourself as a personalized employment service. Part of your job description as manager of this employment service includes prompt post-interview writing. That writing involves three steps: critiquing your interview performance, recording important information, and composing a Thank You letter.

Immediately after your interview, critique your performance in that meeting. While the memory is fresh, write down one thing you did well, such as, "maintained good eye contact, asked an especially insightful question (what was that question?), used a certain element of vocal style effectively (be specific)..." Write down at least one skill or behavior that should be improved. Learn how to improve it. Continually work on improving that skill BEFORE your next interview (which might be a second interview with the company you just visited). For instance, did you forget the interviewer's name? Did you seem to stall while thinking of a story that exemplifies an admirable quality or skill that you have? Why did you say "um" or "ya know" or "like" so many times?

The second of these three steps is record-keeping. *Immediately following your self-critique, write down certain specific details of the interview.* Include the date, time, and place; the name(s) and title(s) of your interviewer(s); specific company needs, specific/detailed contributions which you feel you can make to the company, and any other comments that you consider note-worthy. Not only will these ideas come in handy when you review your journal for networking names and for business ideas in general, but they will also be necessary when you practice the third skill we are discussing...

Sending a handwritten *Thank You letter*. This will separate you from the crowd of other applicants. According to Fuchs and Manning, "only two out of every ten people ever follow up an interview with any written communications." Your letter should have *three concise and basic parts*. First, it should thank the interviewer for his/her time. Next, compliment a specific aspect of the company in a sincere way. Finally, point out precisely how you feel you can be of benefit to the company (this is an ideal time to briefly discuss one of your strengths or qualities which went unmentioned during the interview).

Your letter confirms your interest in the company in general, and that job opening in particular. Your letter also confirms, without you having to say so, that you are unique among interviewees; it says that you are a professional. A letter should go to *each person you interviewed with*. Each letter should be different in content from the other.

These three steps—the performance-critique, the organized keeping of records, and the Thank You letter—can help improve your chances of landing the job you want. Practice these steps during your employment; they can help you better your chances of developing a long-term career that you will be very proud of.

Hints to Remember

- Seek out and encourage feedback on your effectiveness at work.
- Routinely keep a log of accomplishments *as you achieve them*.
- Plan for the unexpected.
- When writing a Thank You letter, write it out in longhand for a more personal touch.

CHAPTER 20

Congratulations . . . But Hold the Phone!

What If You're *Offered* the Job?

If you're offered the job, ask yourself seriously, *is this the job that you really want*? Ask your possible prospective employer, if you don't really know, how soon they want a response. Remember you, too, have been seeking the right place of employment, just as they have been seeking the right employee. You don't just want to consider any vacant position.

Most likely, you won't have much time to think things over, let alone have the luxury to wait for other interviewers to get back to you. So you need to think, act, and think again.

Hopefully, as noted in the preceding chapter, you have kept thorough notes during the interviewing process. Now is the time to consult those notes to remind yourself of this particular opening that is being offered to you so you can make a responsible decision. *List reasons, on paper, why you should accept and why you should reject this offer*. Only you can list the advantages and disadvantages for yourself, depending on your own personal goals and values. If this offer is not your first choice as of yet, *consider your chances of getting that job*. You might also want to make the same assessment of your first choice *now*, because you may feel differently later.

Ask yourself:

- What do I want to do?
- Do I want to work at the job?
- Is there room for advancement?
- Do I like the working environment?
- Would I feel comfortable there? Do I fit in?

- Can I do better financially and are there benefits for me?
- How will this look on my resume?
- What other questions do you have that need answering?
- And, how soon do I start?

As soon as you have made a decision, and one you can clearly live with, communicate that decision to the employer either by telephoning or by writing a letter.

And above all else, enjoy your new job and good luck!

Hints to Remember

- List reasons in favor of, and not in favor of, taking the job.
- Use that list to make an informed, rather than an emotional or hasty, decision.

CHAPTER 21

You Can *Win For Losin'*

What If You're *Not* Offered the Job?

Congratulations! Because you were not offered the job that you interviewed for, you now have another chance to sharpen your job-search skills.

As a job-hunter, you are like an athlete—a runner, for example—who is trying to coach him/herself for the next meet. You must be sure to sharpen your skills, improve your equipment, and bolster your attitude.

In order to refine the necessary skills, a coach and athlete must know the specific skills and behavior which are important, they must know which of those are already strong, and which need improvement.

Consultants Richard Fuchs and Keith Manning identify behaviors dealing with professional appearance, skillful communicating, knowledge of self, and knowledge of target company as examples of critical interview strengths.[1]

In your *job-search notebook*...You DO have one, don't you? If not, start one *now*. Preferably, use a three-ring binder. In it, you can add notes, store copies of correspondence, and file a detailed list of interview-related skills. Also put in a journal section. After each interview write down AT LEAST one thing that you did well, and one thing that you could have done better during that interview. Describe what you will do differently during the next interview, and review your journal the day before that meeting.

Your job-search strategy, or plan, should be considered a group of skills. *Clearly* identify your objective[2] and use a variety of techniques to

---

1. Richard A. Fuchs and Keith A. Manning. *The Successful Job Hunter (Karli and Associates, Inc., 1986), pp. 66, 80, 81.*
2. J. Michael Farr, "Essential Steps for a Successful Job Search," *National Business Employment Weekly*, December 16, 1990, p. 17.

79

find jobs. (DEFINITELY employ networking: at least 70% of all jobs are found through personal contacts.)[3]

Second, your basic equipment should be examined by you *and* by an acquaintance in business. A resume is as basic a piece of equipment to the job-hunter as a pair of sneakers is to a runner. In this case, however, you have an advantage over most runners: you can custom-design your gear, your resume.

This equipment is an advertisement promoting a unique and exceptional "product": YOU. Make sure that it highlights your experiences and achievements which are pertinent to the employer you are applying to. Make sure that its verbal style "sells" you.[4] Your resume's visual style—its professional appearance—should be considered, too.[5]

Suggestion: *contact your last interviewer; ask for a 15-20 minute "informational interview"* in which you ask for that individual's ideas regarding improvements you can make in your interviewing skills, your strategy, your resume, of any other area that he or she may feel is important.[6] Bring a copy of the cover letter, resume, and (if applicable) portfolio which the interviewer looked at during your interview.

Log those recommendations in your notebook and incorporate them into your behavior and paperwork as you see fit.

Finally, and forever, develop and maintain strong self-confidence and a positive attitude. Hugh C. Anderson, President of Hugh Anderson Associates/Outplacement International, says that "attitude can be more important than aptitude and is a primary determinant of job-search success."[7]

Athletes "psyche themselves up" for each meet. In preparation for your next interview, for your job, and for over-all success, you should do the same. Work through each day as though you were at a job—because you ARE; looking for work is a full-time job. Maintain a professional image even (and especially) if you are home at work an your job-search.[8]

---

3. Hugh C. Anderson, "When Procrastination Hinders Your Job Hunt," *National Business Employment Weekly*, January 27, 1991, p. 9.
4. Charles L. Mundell, "The Resume: Advertising Your Ability to Do The Job," *CPC Annual: 1991-1992* (Bethlehem, PA: College Placement Council, Inc., 1990), p. 26.
5. Betty Redfield [Employment Counsellor with the New York State Department of Labor], Interview with Author, January 29, 1991.
6. Redfield Interview with Author.
7. Anderson, "Procrastination," p. 9.
8. Bruce Bradley [Account Executive, Park Communications], Interview with Author, February 12, 1991.

Use language to bolster your morale. Compliment yourself; there is at least one specific action or result which shows good work on your part. Congratulate yourself for that good work.

In facing your challenges, forget the weak question "Can I?" *Ask the assertive, positive, I-know-there's-a-way question* "HOW *can I?*" Find your answer and complete your task.

As you review your journal entries over time, you will notice that skills, equipment, and attitude which needed improvement HAVE improved; you are making positive progress.

Amazing, isn't it? You are in a position of unique potential. As you prepare for upcoming interviews, you are learning about yourself, learning about your field of study, and you are learning certain coaching skills. You are also developing insight into emotions to be shared by others who will someday be in the position that you are in now. Remember the trauma that you are feeling, so that when someone asks *you*, Coach, for help in their search for a job, you can give that help with understanding and sensitivity.[9]

Hints to Remember

- Turn this potentially negative situation into a positive one: contact this interviewer and ask for an "informational interview;" *Learn from this event.*
- Always find an interviewing skill which you can improve on, and always find at least one that you can do well.

---

9. David Hildebrandt [Former Personnel Manager, Addis-Dey Corporation], Interview with Author, February 12, 1991.

PART FIVE

Twists, Tricks, and Special Cases

CHAPTER 22

S.A.T.'s, or Y.O.U.?

The College Transfer Interview

If you are an absolutely outstanding student, with S.A.T. scores over 1450, and straight A's in all of your courses, the college interview will probably not make or break your academic future. Recruiters are deluging you with viewbooks and videos. Every day produces a flurry of glossy mail. If you are one of these fortunate few, read no further. But, if you don't fall into that category, read on.

Like any other interviewing situation, the college transfer interview produces a predictable range of responses—panic, self-complacency, anxiety, placidity, trepidation, confidence, distress. And like any other interviewing situation, you will be far more successful if you prepare.

There are two main types of college interviews. One is the *on-campus interview*, conducted by an admissions officer of the college. The other, far more common situation is the *alumni interview*. One major difference between the alumni interview and the employment interview is that most college interviewers are *not* employed by the college. Most are professionals, living in your town; people who were once where you are now. That almost always puts them in your corner.

Do your homework before you appear at your interview. Find out the name, occupation and background of your interviewer. But don't try too hard to impress the interviewer. As in the employment interview, the interviewers are looking for qualities which will determine your 'fit' with the college. Be prepared to talk about your academic, professional and personal interests. "Tell me about yourself" is probably the best—and the hardest—question you will be asked. Don't be afraid to discuss areas in which you excel, but make sure your interest is genuine. Nobody likes a phony.

Look over your transcript for areas that might raise questions or cause concern. Write out and rehearse answers for questions that may arise. Think about the activities you have participated in. What do they say about you? What kind of a person do they show you to be? Why should the college *want* that type of person?

If possible, arrange a 'mock-interview' with a friend or the parent of a friend. Tape record your answers. How do you sound?

Finally, remember that these interviews work both ways—Colleges today need qualified students as much or more than students need the particular college. Use the interview to find out as much information as you can about the atmosphere of the place. Ask questions. Lots of questions. You'll be the one who'll suffer the consequences if you don't.

Hints to Remember

- Find out as much as you can about the college and the interviewer in advance.
- The interview will tell the college more about you than all the pieces of paper you could possibly send them.
- Look for 'holes' in your application or transcript and be prepared to answer questions about them.

CHAPTER 23

Fake?

The 'Mock,' or Classroom Interview

How do you approach all of the above, when it isn't for real?

Therein lies the problem. It's *always* for real. Even if you are 'just doing it for a grade' (believe it or not, I actually hear students say this in the hall as they are preparing for their interviews), it's *real*.

In a job interview that is part of a career move, you will get a position, and a salary. In a Classroom Interview, you get the skills that will allow you to have a *successful* career interview. Unless you want to have a couple dozen *unsuccessful* "real" interviews, you better take *any* opportunity to practice seriously. Let's face it—practice may not make perfect, but it'll certainly make you *better*.

Still can't get yourself "up" for going to an Instructor's Office, and being interviewed by another Instructor, a Teaching Assistant, or someone whom the Instructor pulled in at the last minute? Try some of these on for size:

1. If the interview is being videotaped, think of it as a *portfolio piece*.

In some fields, you may be able to use the video as a part of your application, to show that you have the stuff that it takes to do the job.

2. Think of it not as a part of any specific course, but *as part of your overall career training*.

Most students say that they want their education to train them to get a job. This is the best way to get ready for this. Why are you complaining about having to do it? This was the type of education that better than eighty percent of high school graduates said that they *wanted*!

    3. Do *not* approach it as a "If I get the job, I get an A; if I blow it, I get an F" experience.

No matter how much the above statement is like the "real world" (and it *is*), no self-respecting teacher will grade a classroom assignment like that. They want to *teach* you from this experience. Therefore . . .

    4. Approach the mock interview as an assignment that will help you to learn a valuable skill, and *do it better the next time* — when it counts.

Hints to Remember

- It's as real as any other interview, so . . .
- Treat it that way.

CHAPTER 24

Abridged Over Troubled Waters:

Using an Art Portfolio

Sparks fly and gears whir as you create a device designed to help you land a job. You pause for a moment, then take step back to study this invention. Relatively long, wide, and narrow, it rests quietly on your laboratory bench. You call it your Art Portfolio.

Like a montage of Leonardo DaVinci/Thomas Edison/Frank Lloyd Wright, you are an inventor, a designer and an artist. And, like these creative people before you, you know that each of your creations must be planned with at least two basic ideas in mind: WHO will be using it, and what is its PURPOSE.

Let's step out of your laboratory and consider the first idea: *who are you designing this portfolio for?* Prospective employers, of course. Consider their needs and wants as you decide what parts to install in this device.

Whether looking for a graphic illustrator, an interior designer, an architect, or any other position in the general field of Art, an employer is usually looking for someone who can perform two functions: 1) immediately tend to jobs requiring basic skills, and 2) creatively solve major problems (after additional training and experience).[1] Therefore, *be sure to exhibit examples of your work which show employers that you are competent and that you have potential for growth.* Display samples which demonstrate your current strengths. Your portfolio becomes like an x-ray machine, letting the interviewer see your backbone of basic skills.

In order to distinguish yourself from other applicants, and in order to highlight the full range of skills you have begun to develop, *include a special-interest project's case history* (in as complete and *concise* a way as possible).[2] At this point, your portfolio is like a time machine, allowing the

---

1. Donald Holden, *Art Career Guide* (New York: Watson-Guptill Publications, 1961), pp. 200–201.
2. Holden, *Art Career Guide*, p. 199.

89

individual to predict how creative a problem-solver you may become. Keep in mind that "quality is more important than quantity."[3] *At most, you should have a total of 15-20 examples.* Those should be your best, the ones you are proudest of.

Also, *"tune" your portfolio for each interview.* Add, delete, or rearrange your samples as necessary. Ensure that your presentation is pertinent to, and appropriate for: the particular interviewer (what, for example, are that person's specific professional interests?), the company (who are its clients, what campaigns are they involved in, what image do they aim for?),[4] the position (interior designer? decorator?, and the occasion (first interview? second?).

Now, what is the ultimate purpose of these creations, your portfolio? The purpose is to help develop an image of yourself as a professional who has strong basic skills and excellent problem solving potential. Your portfolio, in other words, is not only a visual aid, it is also an advertisement. As such, you should design it for maximum effect and impact.[5]

It must not, however, be a gimmick drawing attention to itself. Like any other project, it must demonstrate your understanding of audience, purpose, and cohesiveness. Keep it as straight-forward as possible and make it simple to use. *Organize it into sections* so that it is comfortable to manage and easy to understand.

A critical question at this point is: How do you handle your portfolio during the interview? Answer: You don't. *"Putting the control of the portfolio in the hands of the interviewer is most satisfying to the interviewer — and that's the person you want to please,"* observes Professor Jo Buffalo, Assistant Professor of Art at Cazenovia College.[6] The interviewer can then decide at what point in the interview to look through the portfolio, and at what pace. He or she may speed past certain examples, then dwell on others, asking questions about specific projects. As you observe and listen for what seems to be most important to the interviewer, you can learn about the job. Ask questions based on those observations in order to flesh-out your understanding of the job opening. In this way, your portfolio becomes a learning tool for you. Professor Buffalo summarizes the ideas contained in this discussion of the design and use of portfolios: Aim for conservative professionalism.[7]

3. Holden, *Art Career Guide,* p. 200.
4. Warren Christensen (ed.) *National Directory of Art Internships, 1991–1992* (National Network for Art Placement, 1990), p. 11.
5. Holden, *Art Career Guide,* p. 216.
6. Prof. Jo Buffalo, Assistant Professor of Art, Cazenovia College, Interview with Author, February 13, 1991.
7. Buffalo Interview with Author.

As you return to your laboratory and your portfolio, remember that appropriate behavior and a well-planned portfolio help develop in you a strong and justifiable feeling of self-worth and confidence.[8]

Hints to Remember

- Analyze your "audience" and adapt your portfolio accordingly.
- "Quality is more important that Quantity."
- Ask for comments regarding your portfolio from other knowledgeable and respected sources.

---

8. Buffalo Interview with Author.

CHAPTER 25

A List of Our Most Valuable Hints

After reading all of this, we hope that you've gotten to know us a bit. We like to think of ourselves as practical, rather than theoretical instructors of the interviewing experience. As such, we often find ourselves giving students hints, rather than lectures, on how to put their best foot forward in the job interview.

Since so few interviewing books are written with that in mind, that's why we wrote *this* one.

We thought we might end on the same note, and give you the hint that we each feel is the most important hint for coming out of a job interview with a job. We may have mentioned these hints elsewhere in the text, but repetition is part of a teacher's stock in trade. So . . .

Hint #1

Rehearse. Rehearse with a friend, the parent of a friend, a helpful teacher or professor, a tape recorder, a mirror, or whatever works for you. *Don't go into an interview cold.*

Dr. Kathryn Barbour

Hint #2

Prepare to discuss salary by researching and rehearsing.

Prof. Maryrose Eannace

Hint #3

Prepare! Preparation builds self-confidence. It is composed of knowledge and behavior. Get in the habit of having everything that you need for this excursion *ready the day before.*

Prof. John Suarez

Hint #4

The well-prepared interviewee, then, is a person with a sense of direction, both physical and psychological.

Prof. Carol Radin

Hint #5

Go for a trial run to the interviewer's office and time the distance. Check out parking in the area. Then the day of the interview will go more smoothly and you won't be hit by any last minute snags.

Prof. Margot Papworth

Hint #6

Plan to arrive at your interview destination at least a half-hour early. This will give you time to relax, find the office, and find the restroom.

Prof. Mary Jean Hessig

Hint #7

Don't memorize questions.
Don't memorize answers.
Don't memorize *anything*.
Go in to *talk* to the interviewer, not to spout off a manual . . . not even *our* manual.

Dr. Bob Greene

Hint #8

Tell the truth. Tell the *best* truth you've got, but *always tell the* truth.

Dr. Fred Berg

Hint #9

Try to choose a job that you'll truly enjoy. Making a lot of money may seem like an ultimate goal, but it's not as important as job satisfaction. You spend a large percentage of your life at work, so enjoying what you do is a cornerstone to happiness.

Prof. Ed Rezny

INDEX

Advertisements
    Employment Agency, 8
    Want Ads, 7
Alumni Interview, 85
Anderson, Hugh C., 80
Arrival Time for Interview, 27, 35
Assertiveness, 41, 81

Benefits, Job, 65
Buffalo, Jo, 90

Career, 3–5
Chamber of Commerce, 8
Clothing, 27, 37–39
    and nerves, 35
    Accessories, 38
College Transfer Interview, 85–86
Cologne, 38
Confirmation, Note of, 41
Cover Letter, 21–23, 41, 47, 80
    example of, 24–25
Critique of Interviewee's Performance, 75–76

Dollase, Crome, 33–34, 41–42

Employment Service
    State, 7
    Private, 8
Empowerment, 41–42
Enthusiasm, 56
Equal Opportunity Commission, 62
Eye Contact, 48, 56, 62, 67

Face: See Gestures, Facial
Fair Employment Practices Commission, 61
Fuchs, Richard, 79

Gestures
    Facial, 67–68
    Hands, 67–68

Hair and Hair Style, 38
Handshake, 38, 47
Hygiene, General, 37

Informational Interview, 80
Interviewer, The, 51–54
Interviews
    Alumni Interview, 85
    College Transfer Interview, 85–86
    Informational Interview, 80
    'Mock,' or Classroom Interview, 41, 87–88
    On-Campus Interview, 85

Lawsuit, for Illegal Questions, 62
Listening, 57

Makeup, 37–38
Manning, Keith, 79
'Mock,' or Classroom Interview, 41, 87–88

Nadell, Carol, 34
National Directory of Advertisers, The, 8
Nerves, 33–35, 48, 72
    and Interviewee's Questions, 70
"Networking", 8, 80
Newspapers, 28
Non-Verbal Communication, 56, 67–68
    Colonge, 38
    Eye Contact, 48, 56, 62, 67
    Gestures
        Facial, 67–68
        Hands, 67–68
    Hair and Hair Style, 38
    Handshake, 38, 47
    Hygiene, General, 37
    Makeup, 37–38
    Perfume, 38
    Posture, 68
Notebook, Interviewee's for Job Search, 79

On-Campus Interview, 85

Peale, Norman Vincent, 68
Perfume, 38
Placement Office, College, 7
Portfolio, 80, 87
Portfolio, Art, 89–91
    "Special Interest Project," 89–90
Posture, 68

Questions
    Asked by Interviewee, 42, 69–70
    Asked by the Interviewer, 48, 51–66
    Illegal, 43, 61–62

Reader Evaluation Form, 100–103
Recruiters, 7
References, on a resume, 13
Reilly, Dr. Susan, 33–35
Resume, 11–19, 21, 42, 47, 52–53, 80
    examples of, 15–19
    salary on, 9
Rogers, Henry, 47

Salary, 5, 7–8, 58, 63–66
    on a resume, 9
Scholastic Aptitude Tests (SAT's), 85
Secretaries, conversation with, 27

Self-Assessment, 28–29
Smoking, 37, 48
"Special Interest Project", in Art
    Portfolio, 89–90
Standard and Poors, 8
State Division of Human Rights, 61

Thank-You Letter, 41, 76
Thomas Register, The, 8
Truth, Telling the, 43

Videotaping of Interviews, 66

Written Work for the Interview Situation
    Confirmation, Note of, 41
    Cover Letter, 21–23, 41, 47, 80
        example of, 24–25
    Critique of Interviewee's Performance, 75–76
    Notebook, Interviewee's for Job Search, 79
    Resume, 11–19, 21, 42, 47, 52–53, 80
        examples of, 15–19
        salary on, 9
    Thank-You Letter, 41, 76

Reader Evaluation Form

As we noted in the beginning, we wrote this book for students like yourself. We are *very* interested in your comments, and we hope that you will take the time to write us with your thoughts. We guarantee that your ideas will be included as we update our work for future editions.

Please send this form to:
        "THE QUEST: An Evaluation"
        Cazenovia College
        Box F
        Cazenovia, NY 13035

Thank You!

_____

_____ Freshman _____ Sophomore _____ Junior _____ Senior _____ Grad

_____ Faculty _____ Staff/Administrator _____ Personnel Professional

_____ Other (Please Elaborate Below)

Class in Which *The Quest* Was Used:

School/College/University:

• General "Gut Response" to the Value of the Text:

98 EVALUATION FORM

• The Chapter that helped you the MOST, and WHY:

• The Chapter that helped you the LEAST, and WHY:

• A Topic that is MISSING, and Needs to be ADDED:

• Where You Think We Should EDIT (Too much written on an unimportant point):

• Other Messages or Thoughts to the Authors:

Optional:

Name _____

Address _____

_____